ISBN: 978-1-365-73061-0

Certificate of Registration Number: TX 8-562-051

Table of Content

A special congratulations to YOU!

Congratulations on beginning your business ownership journey. This workbook will encourage you to think about many forgotten aspects of business. We hope you find this tool useful in the planning stage of your business. Congratulations once again on taking that leap of faith into business ownership!

About the Authors

Kimisha James, MBA - RK3A, LLC

Kimisha James, President of RK3A, LLC
bookkeeping and administrative consulting firm.

Kimisha made some not so good choices in her life. She dropped out of college right before her Junior year. She never allowed her not so good choices to hinder her from attaining her dream of business ownership.

Against all odds in 2009 she purchased her first home at the age of 23! She proudly walked across the stage eight months pregnant in 2010 to obtain her Bachelor's degree in Business Management. She also completed her MBA October of 2014 and is currently working on two entrepreneurial projects.

She is ambitious and determined to create generational wealth
for her family
...and YOU can too!!!

Chandra Gore - Chandra Gore Consulting

Chandra Gore, Principal Consultant of Chandra Gore Consulting Business Foundation Consulting Firm.

Chandra's entrepreneurial spirit started at an early age. Working along side her father within his many businesses as well as his colleagues; Chandra was a sponge soaking up the ins and outs of how businesses are started, ran and also sometimes fail or succeed. Using this knowledge at the age of 19 she started her own baking company which blossomed into a full service catering and event planning company. As her friends watched many turned to her for advise on how to start and run their own businesses. Thus began her path into business consulting. Using the knowledge gained from working within Fortune 500 companies as well as the Department of Defense she is able to offer that knowledge to her clients.

Her motto is, "If you start with the right foundation nothing can stop your path to success!"

ICE

BREAKER

EMPLOYEE
VS.
ENTREPRENEUR

In your own words describe the difference between an employee and an entrepreneur.

EMPLOYEE
VS.
ENTREPRENEUR

EMPLOYEE
VS.
ENTREPRENEUR

BUSINESS OWNERSHIP

In your own words what does business ownership mean and
why is business ownership important to you?

BUSINESS OWNERSHIP

BUSINESS OWNERSHIP

CHAPTER ONE

DISCOVERY

WHAT INSPIRES YOU? WHY?

WHAT ARE YOUR INTERESTS?

WHAT IS YOUR IDEAL PRODUCT OR SERVICE YOU WOULD LIKE TO PROVIDE?

CHAPTER TWO

BRAINSTORMING

WRITE DOWN 3-5 IDEAL NAMES FOR YOUR BUSINESS

WHAT DO THOSE BUSINESS NAMES MEAN?

WHAT MESSAGE DOES YOUR BUSINESS NAME CONVEY?

WHO IS YOUR IDEAL TARGET MARKET (THIS QUESTION IS GEARED TOWARDS THINKING ABOUT YOUR TARGET CUSTOMER)?

CHAPTER THREE

MARKETING

HAVE YOU CREATED YOUR PRODUCT OR SERVICE WITH YOUR PREFERRED CUSTOMER IN MIND?

DESCRIBE YOUR BRAND?

HAVE YOU CONDUCTED MARKET RESEARCH?
(THIS QUESTION IS GEARED TOWARDS UNDERSTANDING YOUR COMPETITION)

WHAT METHODS OF COMMUNICATION WILL YOU USE TO REACH YOUR PREFERRED CUSTOMER BASE? (EXAMPLE: SOCIAL MEDIA, EMAIL MARKETING, FACE-TO-FACE NETWORKING)

CHAPTER FOUR

SWOT ANALYSIS

(strengths, weaknesses, opportunities and threats analysis)

WHAT ARE YOUR BUSINESS STRENGTHS? (THINK ADVANTAGES, UNIQUE - LOW COST RESOURCES, UNIQUE SELLING POINT; CONSIDER THE CUSTOMER POINT OF VIEW)

WHAT ARE YOUR BUSINESS WEAKNESSES? (THINK IMPROVEMENTS, THINGS TO AVOID AND FACTORS THAT COULD PREVENT DEAL/SALE CLOSURE)

WHAT OPPORTUNITIES ARE AVAILABLE TO YOUR BUSINESS? (THINK INTERESTING TRENDS, CHANGES IN TECHNOLOGY, CHANGES IN SOCIAL PATTERNS & LIFESTYLE CHANGES)

WHAT THREATS COULD YOUR BUSINESS FACE? (THINK OBSTACLES, COMPETITION, CASH-FLOW AND CHANGES IN SPECIFICATIONS FOR YOUR PRODUCT OR SERVICE)

CHAPTER FIVE

REGISTRATION

IN WHAT STATE(S) WOULD YOU LIKE TO BASE YOUR BUSINESS?

HOW WOULD YOU STRUCTURE YOUR BUSINESS?

ARE YOU FAMILIAR WITH THE FEDERAL, STATE, LOCAL BUSINESS REGISTRATION PROCESS?

HOW DO YOU WANT YOUR BUSINESS FINANCES TO RUN?

CHAPTER SIX

IMPLEMENTATION

WHAT STEPS WILL YOU TAKE TO START YOUR BUSINESS?

HOW DO YOU INTEND TO FUND YOUR BUSINESS?

HOW DO YOU INTEND TO HANDLE YOUR BOOKKEEPING/TAX PREPARATION FOR YOUR BUSINESS?

CHAPTER SEVEN

GOALS

WHAT ARE YOUR FIRST YEAR BUSINESS GOAL(S)?

WHAT DO YOU ASPIRE TO ACCOMPLISH IN THE FIRST 3 YEARS OF BUSINESS?

WHAT DO YOU ASPIRE TO ACCOMPLISH IN THE FIRST 5 YEARS OF BUSINESS?

WHAT DO YOU ASPIRE TO ACCOMPLISH IN THE FIRST 10 YEARS OF BUSINESS?

SAMPLE BUSINESS PLAN
OUTLINE

Sample Business Plan Outline

Cover Sheet

(Should include business name, business logo, name of business principle agents, address, phone number and other relevant contact information)

Table of Contents

Statement of Purpose
(Should speak to the purpose of your business)

The Business
(Should include sub-sections which describe the business in detail, the business market, business competition, business location, business management, business personnel and business funding source(s))

Summary

Sample Business Plan Outline

Cover Sheet

(Should include business name, business logo, name of business principle agents, address, phone number and other relevant contact information)

Sample Business Plan Outline

Table of Contents

Sample Business Plan Outline

Statement of Purpose

(Should speak to the purpose of your business)

Sample Business Plan Outline

The Business

(Should include sub-sections which describe the business in detail, the business market, business competition, business location, business management, business personnel and business funding source(s))

Sample Business Plan Outline

The Business continued.
(Should include sub-sections which describe the business in
detail, the business market, business competition,
business location, business management, business personnel and
business funding source(s))

Sample Business Plan Outline

The Business continued.
(Should include sub-sections which describe the business in detail, the business market, business competition, business location, business management, business personnel and business funding source(s))

Sample Business Plan Outline

Summary

CHAPTER EIGHT

NOTES

Notes

Notes

Notes

Notes

Notes

Notes

THANK YOU

BRINGING YOUR ENTREPRENEURIAL DREAMS TO LIFE